Good People, Bad Things, and Vice Versa

By: Dr. Delron Shirley

Delron Shirley
3210 Cathedral Spires Dr.
Colorado Springs, CO 80904
www.teachallnationsmission.com
teachallnations@msn.com

Table of Contents

Preface

This volume is part of a trilogy of short independent works that are intended to stand alone but should also be read as a series since they have a unifying theme. Good People, Bad Things, and Vice Versa deals with the age-old question of why God allows bad things to happen to good people and good things to happen to bad people; the sequel, A New Dawn Rises, deals with the struggles that we go through as Christians, and the concluding volume, Becoming a Person of Legacy, suggests an approach to living a life that makes a lasting mark in history. The consistent thread that is woven throughout the fiber of each book is the biblical principle that a man is what he thinks about in his heart (Proverbs 23:7) and that we have to determine not to be forced into the mold of thinking like everyone else does (Romans 12:2) – hence, the tile: The Non-Conformer's Trilogy.

As Christians, we often have the simplistic opinion that we live by the New Testament and the Jews live by the Old Testament. However, if you were to investigate the Jewish faith, you would discover that their beliefs and practices are not actually formulated from the Old Testament itself but from the interpretations that the rabbis have given to the Old Testament passages over the centuries. The explanations behind what they believe, the ceremonies they practice, and how they conduct their lives are more likely phrased, "As the rabbis say…" rather than, "In the Bible…"

But, before we point a finger, we need to consider our own lives. I think of one individual that I sometimes discuss biblical ideas with; her standard response is, "Well, that's not what I've always been taught." The truth is that this is not just the reply of one individual; it is the universal reaction of believers in general. Even though it may not be verbalized aloud, this is what actually goes on secretly in our hearts and quietly in our minds. We filter all our opinions and beliefs through the doctrines of our denomination, the lessons of our favorite Bible teachers, and the theology of our culture.

Several years ago, I had the privilege of being part of a team that developed a new discipleship program to be used by Every Home for Christ in their ministry around the world. Once the curriculum was finalized, I was assigned to travel the globe training the national leaders how to implement the new program. North America, South America, the Caribbean, India – no problem. But I encountered something really unanticipated when I got to Africa. One of the lessons is based on Jesus' visit to the home of Mary and Martha – the story about how Martha was busy serving while Mary occupied herself with listening to Jesus teach. Everywhere else in the world, Mary is always considered the heroine of the story because she chose the "good part, which shall not be taken away from her." (Luke 10:42) However, in Africa where women (as you will learn in Good People, Bad Things, and Vice Versa) are expected to serve and not even take a seat at the dining table, Martha became the superstar of the lesson – totally disrupting the lesson plan. It took some really creative maneuvering on my part to get the object of the lesson across to the participants – not to mention, some imaginative persuasion to get them to commit to teach the lesson so that it would communicate the truth it was designed to illustrate.

It was hard work to get those African delegates to take off their "cultural glasses" and read the passage for what it said. But this is not simply an African problem; it's universal. I pray that you will set your "theological glasses" aside as you read the lessons in this trilogy. I have no doubt that you come across a number of ideas or interpretations that don't agree with what you already believe. When you do, I ask that you simply take the time to look at the verses exactly as they are written in the Bible, not as you have heard someone teach them. Then, I would ask that you go just one step further and take some time to pray in the Spirit as you allow your spiritual man to digest those verses. According to I Corinthians 13:1-3 and 14:2, the avenue to understanding the mysteries of God is through speaking in tongues and allowing the Holy Spirit to prophetically unravel those hitherto-undisclosed revelations for you. If you'd like a more complete explanation of how this principle works, I invite you to read the chapter "How Saul of Tarsus Became the Apostle Paul" in my book Maximum Impact.

I challenge you to stop allowing yourself to be conformed to the thinking of the rest of the world and become transformed into the image of Christ by renewing your mind according to what the Bible actually teaches. With these revised perspectives and renewed insights, I believe that you'll become the individual in your generation who leaves behind a definitive godly legacy!

Why?

A terrified look blanketed his face as the tall African young man walked into my office that April morning in 1994. Almost expressionlessly – depicting the state of shock that he was in – he mouthed the words, "I'm an orphan!" No, those words didn't mean at all what you might expect them to mean. He was not introducing himself and trying to curry any advantage by saying that he was disadvantaged by having grown up without parents. Quite the contrary, he had been one of my students for at least two years at the time, and I knew – at least from his application papers and our conversations on campus – that he had an intact family back in Africa and a sister living in Europe. What he was trying to communicate to me that day was that he had just received the news of his parents' massacre in the Rwandan genocide in which the Hutu tribe had raised up in a well-organized attempt to exterminate the Tutsi tribe. Nearly a million helpless victims were brutally hacked to death with machetes in the bloody one-hundred-day rampage that engulfed the nation. A million souls perished simply because they happened to have been born into the wrong tribe.

Later when I had the privilege of visiting Rwanda, I met many of the survivors of the genocide and heard their stories right from their own mouths. Probably the most impossible-to-comprehend accounts came from those who were part of mixed marriages where part of the family was Hutu and the other was Tutsi. Jane, a Tutsi, told me of how she and her husband, a Hutu, had lived happily together for many years and had raised a loving family together in total harmony. That is, until the day that the planned attacks were to be unleashed with the broadcast of a code phrase on the national radio, "It's time to cut down the tall trees." As soon as the cue was given, the nation erupted into pandemonium and a wide-spread bloodbath. Knowing that his life was endangered because he had a Tutsi wife, the husband grabbed the children that looked more like Hutus and fled – leaving Jane and the children that bore more distinctive Tutsi characteristics helpless in the face of the blood-thirsty mobs. Only by a miracle of God's grace was she rescued as the crazed assailants hacked her family members to pieces.

Neither my student nor Jane – nor any of the other almost million victims – deserved what happened during those three months of insanity. They were good people but the most horrible of atrocities were being perpetrated upon them. And our age-old question that must automatically accompany such occurrences is, "Why?"

In my travels around the world, I've met more than my share of good people who have endured the full litany of bad things.

There was Maria who survived a Nazi concentration camp where her family were interned for most of World War II – simply for being friends with their Jewish neighbors. Although Maria was never chosen for any of the "medical research" that used the children in the camps as human guinea pigs, she witnessed what happened to the other boys and girls who shared her barracks. Of course, she endured unspeakable deprivation and watched her parents suffer through inhumane torture and abuse of unspeakable proportion.

There was also Julie who grew up in a fairly happy home in the Democratic Republic of the Congo. By "happy," I don't mean privileged – but, at least, her family had enough to get by on. Her life was hard but bearable as she worked each day on the family farm and had to walk over rough mountainous paths back to the village where her family lived and her father ran the local school. Then came the day, when a handsome young man came and took her away from the farm to the city to become his wife. With a promising career as a teacher, he offered her a bright future and a happy life. One twist in the road toward their bright hope was that her husband had to take a job outside the country. The couple moved to Burundi, but had to leave when civil war broke out. He found a good job in the neighboring country of Rwanda and resettled just in time to have to flee again when the genocide erupted. At that time, the couple returned to their native Congo but were faced with yet another tragic civil war. It seemed as if wars were following them no matter where they tried to settle. The Congo war found Julie – eight-and-a-half-months pregnant – and her toddler living in what became the cross-hairs of the fight between the rebel forces and the military. Their only hope was to escape back to her parent's village – a torturous foot journey for anyone – and especially for a woman just ready to give birth. With a prayer in every breath that she took, Julie miraculously made the grueling days-long trek back to the village where she delivered a healthy baby girl. As the war intensified, the hostilities engulfed the countryside as well as the cities. By this time, the insurgents had added a new element to their terrorizing strategy – humiliating the locals by raping the women. This exploitation was more than just a way to satisfy their own carnal desires; it was a way of crippling the people because it rendered all the women who had been raped as outcasts in their native African culture – thus unraveling the very fiber of the society. Facing this sort of violence in addition to the death and destruction already associated with the fighting, Julie knew that she would have to flee the country all together. Carrying the newborn on her back and with her toddler pulling at her skirt tail, Julie again set out on an impossible journey by foot to escape her war-torn homeland. Eventually, she wound up in a refugee camp without any knowledge of where her husband was and nothing to live on. Food and the basic necessities of life were just not available, but she and her children somehow survived until the Red Cross eventually reunited her with her husband and the United Nations offered them an opportunity to be relocated in the United States. Finally, something good – rather than the litany of bad things that had become the story of her life – seemed to be coming to Julie. Her husband found a good job, they bought a comfortable home in a nice suburban subdivision, she learned English, and their family grew. Then one day, the Lord spoke to them to move to Colorado to go to Bible college – a decision that meant giving up everything that they had accumulated and starting over "from scratch." Of course, that was hard – but it was doable. That is, until tragedy struck again. Julie's husband had a sudden heart attack and died within just a couple days – leaving her with

7

seven children to raise all on her own, debts to pay, school bills to cover, and all the costs of maintaining their home. Again, that haunting question: "Why? How can such bad things happen to such good people?"

Then there was Mark, one of the kindest men you could ever hope to meet. With a military background before going to Bible college, he felt that it was his duty to re-enlist when the Army needed chaplains to serve in the Gulf War following Desert Storm. Leaving his wife and young sons behind, he headed for Iraq to serve his country and to bless our men in uniform as they faced uncertainty, injury, and death on the front lines. Tragically, the horrors that he endured on the field left him crippled with PTSD (Post Traumatic Stress Disorder) – a malady that left him dysfunctional and emotionally incapacitated for years. How can such devastation come to someone whose only intention was to do good and help others?

Of course, there are all degrees of bad things that can happen to good people. I remember growing up in the Deep South where I witnessed parades of white-robed Klu Klux Klan members hiding their identity beneath their hoods while they burned crosses on the fields next to the housing projects where the colored community was ghettoed. In my hometown, there were water fountains with refrigeration units to give a refreshing cool drink – but they were labeled "White only." Beside the water coolers were spigots that came directly out of the plumbing system; they were marked, "Colored." There were three bathrooms at the gas station: "Men," "Women," and "Colored." We had what were called "separate but equal" schools. Of course, there was nothing equal about the quality of the facilities or the education offered inside those "separate" buildings. The idea of a black man entering a café and sitting down to eat next to a white man was unthinkable – a concept that I never understood since most of the cooks were black. It never made sense that a white man could not sit next to a colored man to eat food that had been prepared by a black cook. The most ironic event was when an instructor from the seminary where I studied invited one of the African students to his home for dinner. When the neighbors protested that he should not

8

have welcomed a black man into his home, the professor responded, "He's not black; he's an African." Why did a whole race of people have to suffer just because of their skin color?

When I was ministering in the Congo, one of the church leaders invited me to his home for a meal. His wife offered us a glorious spread of African dishes – obviously, the fruit of hours of hard work. After a formal prayer of thanksgiving, the roomful of guests took our plates and began pile them high with all the delicacies spread out before us. As we found places to sit, I noticed the wife sitting on a bench in the corner without a plate. I spoke to my host and explained that I didn't intent to offend the cultural traditions – however, I would love for the wife to join us as we enjoyed her delicious meal. At that point, she got up, took a plate, and headed to the serving table. Before she scooped up any of the delectable cuisine that she had labored to prepare, she pretended to remember something that needed attention in the kitchen. Setting the empty plate down, she disappeared for the duration of the dinner. As I waited in vain for her to return, I remembered the first time I took my wife to India. When we went to a pastor's home for dinner, I pulled out a chair for my wife to sit next to me at the table. My host's response was that she would not be sitting with us in the dining room but with the women in the kitchen. At which point, I suggested that either she sit with me or I would not be able to join him for the meal. Again, I have to ask why half of the world's population has to suffer just because they were born without a Y chromosome. Skin color or gender doesn't make one person better than another, and there is no reason for good people of any color or gender to endure abuse, neglect, or discrimination. But bad things happen to good people – often because of senseless discrimination.

A Hindu philosopher once said, "Unless you specifically declare that you are not a Hindu, you are a Hindu," – and I've come to believe that all humans really are intrinsically Hindus and that we all instinctively believe in karma. Just think about when anything out of ordinary happens – good or bad – what is your automatic response? I bet it is, "What did I do to deserve this?" In our "Christian Hinduism," we blame or credit so many different things. Maybe it's tithing. If we have been consistent with giving God His ten percent, we tend to want to pat ourselves on the back and say, "Of course, I deserve this blessing; I've been honoring God with my first fruits!" And if we have been slack in this area, we find it easy to point to this negligence – or possibly even outright rebellion – as the cause for the "curse" that has attached itself to our finances. Then we go a step further and point toward "sowing seed" beyond the tithe – or the lack thereof – as either the benefactor or the culprit when good or bad things happen to us. Of course, we often summarize our situation as the result of either our excellent trust in God or not believing strongly enough; our diligent discipline of Bible reading or not "being in the Word enough"; our dedication to renewing our minds or our slackness that allowed doubt and unbelief to creep in; our consistent prayer life or our failure to either pray hard enough, long enough, in the Spirit enough, or with exactly the right wording. And then, if we can't really pinpoint any apparent cause for the "bad karma" in our lives, we can simply blame our ancestors for putting some sort of "generational curse" upon us.

Now don't get me wrong, I believe in tithing, sowing seed, studying the Bible, renewing our minds, prayer, and – as they say – the "whole nine yards" of Christian discipline; however, we have to be more discerning than to just point a ready finger at any of these activities and feel that we have a pat answer for the troubling questions of life. In doing so, we have adopted a works mentality that requires us to earn good things in life. Such an attitude totally negates the beautiful plan of God – the plan of grace in which He gives us His blessings as a free gift.

> *For by grace are ye saved through faith; and that not of yourselves: it is the gift of God: Not of works, lest any man should boast. For we are his workmanship, created in Christ Jesus unto good works, which God hath before ordained that we should walk in them. (Ephesians 2:8-10)*

Notice that this verse confirms that we are to do good works (tithe, sow seeds, read our Bibles, pray, believe); however, these good deeds and disciplines are the outgrowth of what God has done in us through His freely given grace – not the methods through which we earn good things in our lives.

Let's test the good-karma-bad-karma hypothesis against the Bible, and there is no better place to start than at the beginning. Therefore, let's turn to Genesis chapter four and see if this principle holds up in the examination of the lives of the first siblings on the planet. By picking the story of Cain and Abel, we are able to eliminate the "generational curse" argument since there was only one generation prior to the the story of these young men. Since the two boys both shared exactly the same lineage, any "curse" that could have passed down through the bloodline would have affected both boys equally. Thus, according to the "Christian Hinduism" principles that seem to be so prevalent in the church today, there is only one possible reason that the two boys turned out differently – their actions and the "karma" that these actions produced. There are only two actions recorded for each of these boys – the choice of careers that they were to follow and the offering that they presented to the Lord. Cain chose to be a farmer, while Abel opted for a career in livestock. Their career choices essentially determined what offerings they could present when they came to worship the Lord. Some who would look for a reason for Cain's downfall like to point to the fact that he presented a vegetable offering rather than a blood offering as his brother did. As spiritual as this explanation may look on the surface, we have to discount it since God Himself specifically commanded that we give

12

offerings of the fruit of the ground (Leviticus 2:1-16; 6:14-18; 7:9-10; 10:12-13) and the devout Jews obediently tithed on every sprig they harvested (Matthew 23:23, Luke 11:42). Others who recognize that God accepts – or actually requires – vegetable offerings are forced to look a little deeper to find a reason for Cain's disgrace, and they come up with the fact that he made his offering in the process of time (Genesis 4:3) whereas his brother's offering came from the firstlings of his flock (Genesis 4:4). Their implication is that Cain was nonchalant about his offering and gave it "when he got around to it," while Abel was diligent and gave his offering as soon as a kid or lamb was birthed. Of course, we only need to take one step back from the text to see the flaw in this logic. Abel obviously could not make an offering until his livestock had calved. That meant that he had to wait for his original animals to reach maturity, breed, and then go through the gestation period before he could give his first fruits offering. Cain was subject to the same sort of time restraint in the giving of his offering since he had to wait for the right season to plant his seed, then he had to wait for the plants to sprout and grow, and then he had to continue waiting for the harvest to ripen – as Jesus Himself described in Mark 4:28, the process of time. In fact, the reaping of a grain offering would have come in the first year that he started farming; whereas, it would have taken Abel's livestock more than one season to reach sexual maturity before he could breed them. Thus, it is likely that Cain's offering actually preceded Abel's by a year or more – totally invalidating the idea that the timing was a determining factor in God's eyes. The very fact that the biblical account records Cain's offering first may be a suggestion that it actually chronologically predated the blood offering of his brother.

So, what was the real reason for the difference between these two young men? The answer is clearly obvious in verse five, "Unto Cain and to his offering he had not respect." Notice that the issue was with Cain himself, not his actions. Apparently, the problem with Cain's person spilled over into his offering. The prophet Isaiah spoke of this same principle when he said that the abominable condition of the hearts of

13

the people made their sacrifices as if they were offering the lives of humans, the flesh of dogs, and the blood of pigs (Isaiah 66:3), and Jesus Himself taught us that we should not make an offering as long as there are unreconciled differences between us and our brothers (Matthew 5:24). Apparently, Cain was the first example of the biblical principle of a person who does everything right externally but whose heart is distant and separated from the Lord. (Isaiah 29:13, Matthew 15:8, Mark 7:6) In this case – if Cain had bad karma, it was a result of who he was in his heart, not what he did with his actions.

Of course the real "nail in the coffin" of "Christian Hinduism" in this story is that fact that Abel is the one who was killed. Even though he was the brother that God honored, he was the one who became the innocent victim of his brother's murderous rage – a good person to whom a very bad thing happened!

Before we go any further with our study, we have to consider Job – the "poster boy" of good people experiencing bad things. Although Job is repeatedly referred to by God Himself as being "perfect and upright" (Job 1:1, 1:8), those who hold to the "Christian Hinduism" principle that there must have been something – some bad karma – in his life that warranted his misfortune look far and wide for a peg upon which that can hang some blame. They usually come up with what they consider a negative confession in verse twenty-five of chapter three, "The thing which I greatly feared is come upon me, and that which I was afraid of is come unto me." Although many Bible teachers say that Job had lived in a perpetual state of anxiety about the loss of all his goods, there is nothing in the narrative to substantiate such a claim. There is only one thing that is ever mentioned in terms of a concern on Job's part – the possible loss of the physical and spiritual lives of his children.

And his sons went and feasted in their houses, every one his day; and sent and called for their three sisters to eat and to drink with them. And it was so, when the days of their feasting were gone about, that Job sent and sanctified them, and rose up early in the morning, and offered burnt offerings according to the number of them all: for Job said, It may be

14

that my sons have sinned, and cursed God in their hearts. Thus did Job continually. (Job 1:4-5)

Let's notice several things about Job's concern over his children's wellbeing. The first and most obvious one was that he didn't stop with the concern or worry; he proactively intervened. Rather than waiting for something bad to happen and then going into intercession for a remedy, Job made a habit of aggressively arbitrating on their behalf as a precautionary measure. The next thing we must notice is that as soon as Job got the news about the catastrophe that struck his son's home – taking the lives of all his children – Job reacted by falling to the ground and worshiping. (Job 1:20) The scripture goes on to say that in all this calamity Job did not sin or blame God foolishly. (Job 1:22) In essence, Job did have a concern – one that was of gargantuan proportions. But there was nothing unhealthy about his concern; it was the natural concern that any godly parent should have for his or her children. Furthermore, the way that he handled his concern was totally appropriate. He was not – as we would say today – a "helicopter parent," hovering over his children nagging them about his apprehension. Instead, he took his worry directly to God. When the thing that he had greatly feared became a reality, he did not accuse God of having failed him; instead, he fell on his face and worshipped God – recognizing that God had not forsaken him or his request. Even though Job didn't understand what was going on, he trusted God through the entire ordeal. So, if he did have some "bad karma" because of his fears and concerns, the "good karma" that he assimilated through his positive actions and attitudes would have more than canceled out his "bad karma."

Again, we have to totally discredit the natural response to look at our actions to find a reason for the good or bad things that happen in our lives. "Christian Hinduism" cannot coexist with biblical Christianity!

One of my friends tells the story of how his father often promised him things and somehow failed to come through, but the most traumatizing event was the day that he sat at home all day waiting for his dad to show up to take him to the circus. When nightfall came, and the father had not shown up, the little boy's heart was broken – not because of anything he did, but totally because of someone else's lack of responsibility.

In my trophy shelf sits a fifty-billion-dollar note from the African nation of Zimbabwe – a reminder of the suffering that devastated the country when uncontrolled inflation destroyed their economy. With an inflation rate of thousands of percents, the money and bank accounts of the people became totally worthless. Many of my friends in the country had worked their whole lives to save up a "nest egg" for retirement – only to have what should have been enough to live on for years barely pay for a week's worth of groceries. These were good, honest Christian people, but they lost everything they had worked their whole lives for because of someone else's greed and inadequate economic policies.

Certainly we all know praying parents whose hearts are broken by prodigal children who go exactly the opposite way from how they were raised. One couple who are close friends of ours had a beautiful daughter who was a dedicated Christian young lady – even pursuing a Bible college degree – yet she came home one day with the announcement that she was pregnant. The parents loved her and were careful to protect her dignity and respect in spite of her condition. The baby was born, and the grandparents sacrificially covered the cost of a new member in their family. The daughter then turned her back on all that she had once stood for, moved out of the house, and started a career in the legalized recreational marijuana business. The parents' world essentially "caved in around them" – not from any fault of their own, but totally because of the poor choices of their wayward daughter.

We all know that slavery was abolished more than a century ago, but the fact is that there are actually more slaves in the world today than at the peak of the slave trade that brought thousands of Africans to the Americas. Today we use the term "human trafficking," but the meaning is the same – someone is forced into a life of servitude and humiliation. I know a couple of those individuals who were snatched away to a less-than-human life of essentially "pack animals" for others. And the most tragic thing about the two individuals that I have in mind as I write is that both were slaves in the homes of their own relatives. It is amazing how parallel their stories are – one, a young boy in Sri Lanka; the other, a young girl in Nigeria; both from poor families that could not support all the children. In both cases, the parents thought that they could give their children a better life if they asked an uncle to adopt just one out of their brood so they would have enough to properly care for the rest. The only thing that they did not know was that in both cases, the uncle saw the new youngster in the home as free help. Cooking, cleaning, laundry, farming, peddling goods on the street corner – there was no end to the demands that the cruel uncles placed upon these tender little children. In return, they got only the scraps that were left after the family had finished their meals, they had no proper bed to sleep in, and they wore only tattered clothes that had been thrown away by their cousins – essentially rags. These innocent children suffered horribly because of no fault of their own; but rather because of the poverty of their natural families and the cruelty and inhumane greed of their heartless uncles.

These are just a few cases out of a litany of stories I could tell that prove just one point – we can't blame karma when bad things happen to good people. These individuals all suffered tragic lives but did nothing to deserve their plight. It is because life is filled with stories like these – and even more heartbreaking ones – that Hindu philosophers invented the idea of reincarnation, or transmigration of souls. When they couldn't find a sufficient reason for the suffering that was all too real in the lives of innocent individuals, they simply made up the excuse that their present suffering was the result of some bad things that they had done in previous lives. This life was their second – or possibly, one hundredth or one thousandth – chance to make things right. Of course, such an idea is totally contrary to the Bible, "It is appointed unto men once to die, but after this the judgment." (Hebrews 9:27) One lifetime and one judgment – not multiple chances – that's all we are promised. Therefore, we have to decide that when bad things happen to good people who have not done anything to deserve it that it's best to put the blame where it belongs – on the evil perpetrators. Unfortunately, it seems to be a human tendency to add insult to injury by trying to blame ourselves – just like the Hindus do – even when we have to make up a reason to pin the guilt on ourselves.

My wife does a lot of counseling with women who have been verbally, physically, and sexually abused – including incest cases. And one of the amazing things that she discovers time and time again as she works with these battered women is that they continue to say that they somehow feel that what has happened to them was their fault. Many of them feel that they weren't pretty enough, that they were too fat, that they weren't smart enough – and the list goes on and on. We have also seen the same guilt complex manifest itself in children whose parents divorce. In some strange way, the children – totally overlooking the faults of the parents – often adopt the blame and assume that the family could have stayed intact if they had not been part of the equation. Of course, all such thoughts are simply deceptions that eat away at the victims from the inside while the external abuse is working to destroy them from the outside.

Let's take a look at a biblical example to get a godly perspective on such situations. If Joseph of the Old Testament had any fault that brought on the calamities in his life, it was nothing more than naivety. When he had the dreams that his brothers would bow down before him, he was just too childish in his thinking to realize that – as the policeman warns during an arrest – anything you say can and will be used against you. He could have saved the whole tragic story that determined his entire young adulthood by simply following the simple pattern that Mary in the New Testament did – to keep all the revelations private and ponder them in his heart. (Luke 2:19) Before you jump ahead of me and say that the things that happened in Joseph's life were all part of a divinely orchestrated plan, allow me to ask one simple question, "Couldn't God have gotten Joseph into Pharaoh's court some other way?" I would suggest that the Creator God had many other creative – and less painful – strategies for fulfilling the destiny that He had for this young man to save the world from the ravages of the seven-year famine.

Now, back to the story. Jealousy drove his brothers to plot his death. Greed caused them to alter their course and sell him as a slave. Vanity forced Potiphar's wife to entrap him when he shunned her advances. Pride – the need to protect his station in life, the desire to preserve his wife's dignity, and the necessity to look like a hero – dictated that his master throw Joseph into prison without a trial. Selfishness ordained that the butler forget his promise to arrange for his release. Joseph suffered in the pit, in Potiphar's house, and in the prison because of other people and their self-gratifying schemes; yet, he came through it all with "flying colors." How? In two different dialogues that he had with his brothers, we see that Joseph had a very powerful internal resource that he was able to draw upon when bad things happened to him. The first conversation was at the point when he revealed his identity to his brothers. Knowing that they would be overwhelmed with the guilt of their despicable deeds, Joseph immediately defused their concerns by saying that in spite of their evil intentions God had used their horrid plot for good. (Genesis 45:4-8) After their father's death, the brothers felt in jeopardy, fearing that the only reason Joseph had shown them favor was the presence of their father. Again, Joseph repeated his heartfelt conviction – that God was working in his favor, no matter how evil the intentions of others were against him. Furthermore, he purposed to do good to them even though they actually deserved judgment. (Genesis 50:19-21) Centuries later, the Apostle Paul would describe what must have gone on inside of Joseph when he penned the words, "Whatsoever things are true, whatsoever things are honest, whatsoever things are just, whatsoever things are pure, whatsoever things are lovely, whatsoever things are of good report; if there be any virtue, and if there be any praise, think on these things." (Philippians 4:8)

Joseph made a determinate decision as to what he allowed in his mind. Apparently, his thoughts must have been filtered through the same eight criteria that Paul listed here – conditions that must be met before any thought qualifies to be meditated upon. It was true that his brothers had plotted to kill him and that they had sold him into slavery; however, simply because those were facts was not sufficient reason to make these thoughts eligible to become part of Joseph's thinking process. He had to find something else factual to focus his attention upon – the fact that God used his being in Egypt as a way to save lives. According to Paul's formula, once a thought passes the truth filter, it then must be subjected to the filter of justice and the honesty filter. What his brothers did to him was the farthest thing from just or honest; therefore, there was no place in his mind for such thoughts. Instead, Joseph had to find thoughts that qualified – the happy homes throughout Egypt and the surrounding area where there was food for the parents to set before their children every day. Next comes the purity filter, then the filter of loveliness, the good-report filter, the virtue filter, and the praiseworthiness filter. Obviously, the diabolical plot of his brothers couldn't pass through any of these filters – thus, Joseph had to find something else to occupy his thoughts while he languished in the bondage of Potiphar's house and in the captivity of the prison. The fact that he prospered in the service of Potiphar and eventually found himself in charge of his master's affairs to the point that Potiphar didn't even feel that he needed to keep tabs on the business (Genesis 39:6) testifies to the fact that Joseph did not sit around moping about his terrible plight in life; apparently, he was thinking of noble things that made his life productive and brought profit and prosperity to his master. We also see the same thing in the jail where the warden committed all the internal working in the prison to Joseph and didn't feel that he need to check behind him (Genesis 39:23) – obviously, not the kind of thing that happens to an inmate who spends his time sitting in his cell consumed with the thoughts of the injustices that have been carried out against him.

Allow me to close this section by making a quick reference back to the innocent victims that I introduced to you in the beginning of this chapter – the boy who missed the circus, the victims of the out-of-control inflation in Zimbabwe, the parents of the prodigal daughter, and the two individuals who grew up in slavery. I just want to comment that they are all living happy, productive lives today because they each one determined to not allow their negative external situations to control their internal lives. Instead, they held firm to hope and faith and always determined to see the hand of God at work in their situations. When bad things happened because of others; there is always the promise that good things can happen because of God!

Have you ever noticed how it's always the Democrats or Republicans who are at fault? We always want to blame the President – and always without even giving him the respect of prefacing his name with the title "President" or even "Mr." It's just "Clinton" or "Bush" or "Obama" or "Trump" who has created all our woes. In fact, President Harry S. Truman kept a plaque engraved with the words "The buck stops here," on his desk as a constant reminder that he needed to take the blame for all the troubles in the country. He knew that if he didn't accept it willingly, the blame would be forced upon him anyway.

Actually, governments and political forces really are a major reason that good people suffer bad things. Just think back to the individuals I introduced in the opening chapter. My student and Jane from Rwanda, Maria in the Nazi concentration camp, Julie in the Congolese civil war – all their pain was inflicted because of governments or forces instigated by attempts to change governments. My mission work has taken me to literally the ends of the earth where I have witnessed every kind of possible suffering as a result of governmental abuses.

I was in Leningrad, Russia, prior to the collapse of the Iron Curtain and witnessed the depraved condition of the people. There were long lines – usually a couple of blocks long – outside each little shop as the people hoped to be able to get enough food to feed their families for the day. Walking around the lines, I would look into the windows of the shops to see that they had almost nothing on the shelves – meaning that only the first few people in line would be able to get anything and the rest would have to go home hungry. When I revisited the same city – by then known as St. Petersburg – after the fall of Communism, I found a thriving economy where there was an abundance of everything. There was no comparison between the impoverished city where people lacked the basis necessities and the new city where every imaginable luxury was readily available. The difference was that there was a new government with a new mindset and a new concern for the citizenry.

In a Muslim-dominated area of Africa, I met a young lady who had been branded as an "enemy of the state" because of her evangelical Christian activity. Sentenced to death before a firing squad, she was lined up with several other convicted "political criminals." When the triggers were pulled, the bullet intended to take her life miraculously missed its intended target; however, she fell to the ground with all the other victims and pretended that the bullet had done its assigned job. For the rest of the day, she lay motionless in a pile of corpses that had been thrown very unceremoniously into a mass grave. Only after nightfall was she able to slip away under the cover of darkness.

Although I have personally never found myself in such a life-or-death situation, I have had many instances where anti-Christian governments have "played their hand" against me. In one Asian nation where religious freedom is technically part of the constitution, the officials have to grant me permission to hold pastors' conferences; however, they still have the right to determine <u>when</u> they will sign off on the official documents. I have arrived in the country not knowing for sure if the endorsement had actually been issued. Of course, they would always grant the permission – at the last minute – when it was too late for any of the out-of-town delegates to make arrangements to attend the meetings. Even with the proper authorization to conduct the meetings, we keep the windows tightly shut and the curtains drawn so that no one on the street can register a complaint about the Christian activity inside the building. Even the leader of the meetings is cautious about being seen with the "outsider" in public. He always enters the building through a different door from the one I use, knowing that even a glimpse of him with the Western Christian will result in a visit from the authorities and a grueling interrogation as soon as I am out of the country. In another Asian country, where we also have to make sure to keep the doors and windows tightly closed, the Christians have to move the venues of their church meetings, Bible studies, and prayer sessions on a regular basis to avoid being raided and arrested.

My work in Nepal began just as the government was going through a reformation process – shifting from a Hindu state to a democratic nation. Prior to that time, the nation was ruled by a king who was considered to be not just a human dignitary but actually a divine ruler in that he was seen as the reincarnation of the Hindu god Vishnu. In a country that was supposedly ruled by an actual deity, any religion other than Hinduism was totally outlawed. Since Siddhartha Gautama was born in Nepal and since the religion he founded is similar to Hinduism in many ways, Buddhism was accepted and actually revered; however, Christianity was considered an alien threat and was heavily persecuted. All Christians who came to do humanitarian work in the country had to sign non-proselytizing contracts which gave them the right to run schools and clinics in the country as long as they didn't share their faith. Any violation of this contract could get them thrown into prison or kicked out of the country. The few national believers in Nepal were subject to constant danger, and I got to know many who had spent time in prison, who had lost their jobs, and who had been beaten for their stance as Christians. Under the influence of the Hindu government, the persecution filtered into all levels of society – including the families. Many of my friends in the country told me of being kicked out of their homes because they had accepted Christ. The face of one woman who always sat on the front row in the services – clapping, dancing, and praising God with all her heart – was terribly disfigured. At first, I assumed that her deformity was the result of leprosy since that disease was prevalent in the nation at that time. One day I asked the pastor about her, and he explained that the scars were the result of her husband having thrown battery acid in her face when he discovered that she had been attending Christian meetings.

I have also spent time in the nation of Hungary where I met many believers who lived through the years of the Nazi occupation and then suffered through decades of Communist oppression. Their stories of imprisonment, depravity, and tyranny are too horrid to repeat, but I will share just one little snippet from the life of one friend who was miraculously saved just hours before the secret police were to come for him and his family. Because he was outspoken about his faith, the government had confiscated his property, taken away his passport, and placed him on their active "watch list." Supporting his family as best as he could by doing handyman jobs in the city, he found work one day painting a house in one of the high-rent districts of town. In what seemed like an "out of the blue" question, the lady of the house asked him if he had a passport. When he answered that he did not, she replied that he should bring all the documentation and photos for his family members when he came to work the next day. It turned out that the lady's husband was the head of the passport office, and she was able to convince him to issue valid travel documents for my friend and his family. When he received the papers, he and his family immediately fled the country. Later, he discovered that his name was at the very top of the list that the government had intended to "detain," a term that meant to be brought into the House of Terror in Budapest – a large facility on the banks of the Danube River where he would be interrogated, subjected to a mock trial, tortured to the breaking point, and forced to make a confession. Then, he would be hanged and his corpse ground to powder and tossed through shoot that dumped the remains into the river – never to be heard of again.

And then, there was my friend who lived through Idi Amin's reign of terror in Uganda, followed by the equally horrible Milton Obote regime. His stories of the "disappearance" of his father and mother, the confiscation of his business, the destruction of the entire social structure, and the unfathomable bloodshed make you wonder how any human can even think of such atrocities – much less, actually execute them upon other humans.

Of course, the Bible is full of examples of the sufferings that result when evil people gain power and control. Pharaoh demanded that every male Hebrew baby be fed to the crocodiles. (Exodus 1:22) The governors in Babylon tossed Daniel to the lions (Daniel 6:15-16), and the king threw Daniel's three companions in the fiery furnace (Daniel 3:19-22). The king of Persia allowed one of his top nobles to convince him to exterminate the entire Jewish population throughout all hundred and twenty-seven provinces of the kingdom. (Esther 3:8-12) Queen Athaliah massacred everyone she chose – including her own children and grandchildren. (II Kings 11:1) Jezebel set in motion a strategy to slaughter all of God's prophets. (I Kings 18:4) King Herod decreed that every male baby in the Bethlehem region be ripped from his mother's arms and butchered before her eyes. (Matthew 2:16)

The list of evil biblical rulers who inflicted suffering upon the good people under their authority could go on and on; however, there is just one thing that I want to point out here, "When the righteous are in authority, the people rejoice: but when the wicked beareth rule, the people mourn." (Proverbs 29:2) The bottom line is that good people will suffer bad things as long as evil men and women remain in political power. Understanding this principle and seeing how that every government in the world is in the hands of people of varying degrees of corruption and malicious intent, we must ask one simple question, "What can we do? What must we do?"

The Apostle Paul gives us one simple answer, "I exhort therefore, that, first of all, supplications, prayers, intercessions, and giving of thanks, be made for all men; For kings, and for all that are in authority; that we may lead a quiet and peaceable life in all godliness and honesty." (I Timothy 2:2)

Notice the multiplied commands – not just prayer, but supplications, intercessions, and thanksgiving. Let's take a few minutes to dissect the apostle's directive to see exactly what he was trying to say to us. Supplication speaks of making humble – but persistent – requests. In essence, such prayers are not demanding prayers like John and James intended to unleash upon the Samaritans by calling fire to consume them when they did not welcome Jesus. (Luke 9:52-54) No wonder they they were nicknamed, "the sons of thunder"! (Mark 3:17) Although we have no record of the prayers that Joseph prayed while in the pit, in Potiphar's house, or in the prison, there certainly was no indication that he wanted lightning bolts to strike down anyone.

27

Alternately, he must have prayed prayers of supplication for everyone who had wronged him. Otherwise, it would have been impossible for him to later face them with such a gracious and forgiving attitude.

Notice that the next command was that prayers be offered for – not about – all men. There is a world of difference in praying for someone as opposed to praying about him. I experienced this principle in a very dramatic way during my doctoral studies. My lead professor – who was supposed to be my mentor – turned out to be my tormentor. Without going into details, let me just make the point that he made my life and experience in the seminary miserable. As you can imagine, I spent a good bit of time praying about the situation – until the day that I got a glimpse into the professor's personal life. When I realized some of the things that he was going through, I began to pray for him and the situation in his life rather than about how he was affecting me. Almost instantly, things made a total turn-about and I began to experience – as Paul expressed it – "a quiet and peaceable life in all godliness and honesty."

Intercession is when we pray for others and their needs with the same intensity that we would for ourselves and our own needs. When we realize that the souls of those who oppress us are destined to a Christless eternity in hell, any suffering that we may be experiencing will pale in comparison – a compelling reason to intercede for even our enemies. (Matthew 5:44, Luke 6:28)

Finally, the apostle commanded that our prayers be with thanksgiving. I seriously doubt that he anticipated that we would give thanks for the bad things that are happening in our lives; however, there is always something to be thankful for in that God is giving us the grace to go through the situation. At this point, I need to share a little story that isn't related to political persecution but it does make a point about the power of thanksgiving. A lady came to me complaining about how she never seemed to be able to "make the ends meet" with her income. When I asked her how many times she had sent her children to school without breakfast, she replied that she had never had to do that. Then I asked if she had ever sent them to school without shoes or proper clothing. Her response was again that she had not had to do so. I then told her to try a little experiment – thank God for the breakfast, shoes, and clothes that she did have rather than to complain about the things that she didn't have. Today, that woman is a millionaire! God enlarged the little that she had in her hand exactly the same way that He multiplied the fish and loaves on the shores of the Galilee. When the disciples looked at the fish and bread, they saw a problem, "There is a lad here, which hath five barley loaves, and two small fishes: but what are they among so many?" (John 6:9) Jesus, on the other hand, gave thanks rather than a complaint and saw the miracle that fed thousands and wound up with much more left over than what he started out with! (John 6:11-13)

I'd like to conclude this section with a personal story from the Himalayan country of Nepal. During a major portion of the two and a half decades that I have ministered in that nation, there was a violent insurgency by the Maoists who were wanting to take over the government. There was much violence, abundance of bloodshed, and constant disruption in every area of life. We never knew when the insurgents would call a strike and shut down all the businesses, stop all transportation, and cut the supply lines that brought food and goods into the country. My team and I were caught in the middle of such strikes on several occasions; one time, I even had to have an escort of six armed guards to get me from the airport to the hotel. When I encouraged the people of Nepal to pray _for_ rather than _about_ the Maoists, the entire political climate began to shift. Finally, the government and the rebels came to a compromise in which the government accepted the demands that the Maoists wanted to present and the Maoists acknowledged that they could work within the existing government without feeling that that had to totally take over the country. The ultimate concession was that the government allowed the Maoists to be recognized as a legitimate political part and gave them the right to field candidates in the regular elections and hold as many positions in the local and national governments as the voters gave them. But here is the icing on the cake: the final

29

negotiations between the governmental leaders and the leaders of the Maoist party and the final signing of the agreement between them took place in the very hotel where I was staying – just two doors down from my room! I will always feel that it was God's little way of letting me know that He appreciated the counsel that I had given to the good people of Nepal who had suffered bad things at the hand of the Maoists.

The humanitarian aspect of my missionary work has taken me around the world in relief projects associated with every kind of natural disaster short of a volcano eruption. I've seen firsthand what the insurance companies refer to as the "acts of God" – a legal term used throughout the English-speaking world to speak of natural hazards outside human control, for which no individual person or government can be held responsible.

I was part of a relief team in Nicaragua after the landfall of Hurricane Mitch, the second-deadliest Atlantic hurricane on record. The team arrived by ship but were unable to dock in the harbor because the waterfront was blocked by ships that had been sunk during the storm. As we distributed food and supplies to the churches, I was amazed to find that at least one church was actively collecting donations to fill shoeboxes for the Samaritan's Purse Christmas project. What a demonstration of the love of God – the Nicaraguan believers were actively helping others in the midst of their own need!

I also had the opportunity to visit the southern coast of India and the island nation of Sri Lanka just weeks after the deadly tsunami of December 26, 2004. As we drove for hours, covering hundreds of miles, we found no relief from the devastation. There was seemingly endless destruction and rubble. No matter how far we drove, the landscape remained the same – heaps of debris and splintered remains of what was once the homes of the people whose lives had come to tragic ends in a split second. I was on the battlefield of nature versus mankind, and – from all I could see – the brutality of nature had vanquished. This overwhelming scene of destruction left an indelible mark on my memory, but it also began to drive me on a quest to understand the implications of the biblical proclamation, "When the enemy shall come in like a flood, the Spirit of the LORD shall lift up a standard against him." (Isaiah 59:19)

Though some recognized Bible teachers have suggested that the comma in this verse be relocated so that the phrase "like a flood" is associated with the moving of the Spirit, it seems natural from the grammatical structure of the sentence that the traditional reading is true to the prophet's original intent when he penned the words. By using a simile (a grammatical expression using "like" or "as" in its description) when referring to the action of the enemy and a metaphor (a comparison without the use of "like" or "as") when describing the response from the Spirit of the Lord, he's linking the two together in a comparison and a contrast at the same time. The attack of the enemy is as devastating as a flood and as unimaginably far-reaching as a tsunami. However – and this is the most important "however" one could possibly commit to paper – when the tsunami strikes, the Spirit of the Lord <u>will</u> raise up a standard against that attack!

To understand what this verse is intended to communicate, we need a bit of a history lesson to accompany the grammar lesson we have just completed. In Exodus chapter seventeen we find the story of a vicious battle between the Israelites and the Amalekites in which the deciding element was the fact that Moses was able to hold his hands up during the entire fray. At any point that his hands began to lower, the enemy began to prevail; when his hands were again raised, the tide turned in favor of the Israelites. With the help of Aaron and Hur, Moses was able to hold his position until his army victoriously took the field. This raising of an ensign over a battle to encourage the combatants and ensure their victory is exactly what the passage in Isaiah is promising. It refers to the same courage-building inspiration that rose up in the heart of Francis Scott Key when he looked through the smoke and fog to see Old Glory still unfurled above the ramparts of Fort McHenry, prompting him to put pen to paper birthing those immortal words, "Oh, say, does that star-spangled banner yet wave…"

But what does that have to do with a tsunami? Well, in my investigations following the inundation, I ran across some incredibly powerful stories of Christians who were saved during this onslaught from the enemy. One pastor told me of driving down the coastal road literally feet beyond the reach of the tsunami's wave as it lashed into shore. Since it was a Sunday morning the day after Christmas, he had changed his normal routine in order to be part of a special service in which the bishop was to deliver a holiday message. Had he been on his normal schedule, he would have further down the road – and well within reach of the inundating wave – at the time the tsunami hit. One entire Christian community was spared because the preacher preached too long. Again, because of the Christmas holiday, there was a guest minister in the area and all the Christians had gathered at one central church a bit inland for his message. Had he not been there, the Christians in the seaside village would have worshipped in their local church and been back in their homes when the massive wave of death attacked. Additionally, had the guest minister stuck with the traditional timetable for worship services, he would have dismissed the people and sent them back down the sandy paths to their homes just in time to have been swallowed up by the churning waters; however, he continued to add more and more points to his message until it went far beyond the usual dismissal time – but just long enough to keep the worshippers on high ground until the tsunami's waters washed back out to sea.

I don't intend to say that no Christians lost lives, loved ones, or livelihoods. By no means is this the case. Even those in the story I just shared came back to find their homes wiped away and their fishing boats splintered. Other Christians did die while some watched as their family members disappeared in the churn of the monstrous waves. They were in no way immune to the tragedy. My only point here is that as the flood was coming in, the Spirit of the Lord was indeed raising up a standard – a victory banner – on behalf of the people of God.

April 25, 2015, was a Saturday morning in Nepal – meaning that it was the time that the Christians were all in church. No, they are not all Seventh Day Adventist; it's just that Saturday is the only day that most Nepalese have off work, making it the most convenient day of the week for them to gather for worship. And it was during the middle of worship time that the tragic 8.1-magnitude earthquake struck. Because of my long-standing relationship with the believers in the country, I rushed into Nepal as soon as possible and initiated an effort to help rebuild churches and homes. As I traveled around the country, I heard many stories of what had happened that Saturday morning. For some, it was a blessing that they were in church since their homes were destroyed but it turned out that the church building proved strong enough to withstand the quake. For others it was a tragedy that they were in church because the building collapsed, killing all the worshippers inside. In fact, I learned of one village that lost the entire Christian population in the matter of the few seconds that it took the church to crumble.

I was in Liberia during the Ebola epidemic that took close to five thousand lives, and I found that the disease did not discriminate between believers and non-believers; however, again and again, I heard stories of Christians who bravely put their own lives at risk to help those infected with the virus and how God protected them.

I have also personally had to deal with so-called "acts of God" that threatened my personal property. I spent the first twenty-five years of my married life in Indiana – in "tornado alley." And eventually, the reputation of our community caught up with us. A tornado touched down in my neighborhood, sending eighty-mile-an-hour winds down my block. A giant tree in one of my neighbor's yards crashed into his house – leaving him with not a split-level home, but simply a split home. The neighbor on the other side had a huge tree fall directly on top of his car – talk about a "compact car." At my house, we lost a lot of limbs and some massive trees, but the only thing that happened to the house itself was that one limb hit the rain gutter as it flew by the back of the house – leaving a one-inch dent in the downspout. When we moved to Colorado, we were no longer threatened by tornadoes; however, we did move into a high wild-fire zone – and that threat eventually made itself real. One Saturday, we were away on a fun day with the family when we got a call telling us that a huge wildfire had broken out essentially in our backyard and that we had only thirty minutes to evacuate. Since we couldn't even get back to the house in thirty minutes, we simply resigned ourselves to the fact that everything we owned was in God's hands and that we could start all over if necessary. For the next seven days, we were evacuated from our home and left with only the clothes on our backs. Just as the ravaging fire – pushed by sixty-mile-an-hour winds – was actually moving into our subdivision, the winds shifted and sent the blaze into another subdivision where almost four hundred homes went up in flames. I can't say anything about the losses that the people – believers and non-believers alike – suffered. However, I can simply say that I believe that God protected my home from the tornado and the fire because I've believed in Psalm 91:10, "There shall no evil befall thee, neither shall any plague come nigh thy dwelling" – a scriptural truth that I've claimed even before I had my own home to apply it to!

Even though we speak of these natural disasters as "acts of God," we know that it is totally contrary to nature of a good God who gives good gifts (James 1:17) to send such calamities upon the earth. In that case, why do they come? Paul gives us an answer when he explains that whole creation literally groans and travails in pain (Romans 8:22) as it waits for the manifestation of the sons of God (Romans 8:19) Certainly, there is an eschatological message – explaining some relevant truths about the end of the world – to be found here; however, it is very important that we actually read these passages in the bigger context. When we do so, we'll readily see that the idea of the turmoil that the created order is experiencing is actually in the context of the necessity for Christians to learn how to live in the Spirit.

> *The Spirit itself beareth witness with our spirit, that we are the children of God: And if children, then heirs; heirs of God, and joint-heirs with Christ; if so be that we suffer with him, that we may be also glorified together. For I reckon that the sufferings of this present time are not worthy to be compared with the glory which shall be revealed in us. For the earnest expectation of the creature waiteth for the manifestation of the sons of God. For the creature was made subject to vanity, not willingly, but by reason of him who*

hath subjected the same in hope, Because the creature itself also shall be delivered from the bondage of corruption into the glorious liberty of the children of God. For we know that the whole creation groaneth and travaileth in pain together until now. And not only they, but ourselves also, which have the firstfruits of the Spirit, even we ourselves groan within ourselves, waiting for the adoption, to wit, the redemption of our body...Likewise the Spirit also helpeth our infirmities: for we know not what we should pray for as we ought: but the Spirit itself maketh intercession for us with groanings which cannot be uttered. And he that searcheth the hearts knoweth what is the mind of the Spirit, because he maketh intercession for the saints according to the will of God. And we know that all things work together for good to them that love God, to them who are the called according to his purpose. For whom he did foreknow, he also did predestinate to be conformed to the image of his Son, that he might be the firstborn among many brethren. Moreover whom he did predestinate, them he also called: and whom he called, them he also justified: and whom he justified, them he also glorified. What shall we then say to these things? If God be for us, who can be against us? (Romans 8:16-31)

The apostle begins this section with the fact that the Holy Spirit is trying to reveal to us that we are the children of God. Then he mentions that the creation is in travail as it anticipates the revelation of the sons of God. Even though this revelation may speak of a future event, the context clearly implies that such a manifestation could come at any point that we as believers actually grasp hold of the message that the Holy spirit is trying to awaken inside of us. Next, Paul reminds us that we have infirmities that keep us from tapping into the realities that God has for us; however, he immediately offers the remedy – the Holy Spirit will direct our prayers with the end result that everything will work out for our good. He then concludes the discussion with the rhetorical question of what opposition could dissuade us when we have this revelation. In other words, Paul is telling us that there is a lot of natural turmoil in the fallen world that we live in and the only way to overcome it is to realize that "Ye are of God, little children, and have overcome them: because greater is he that is in you, than he that is in the world." (I John 4:4)

The Old Testament story of Naomi is a perfect illustration of a woman who lived through a number of "acts of God" and finally found the key to overcoming them. The introductory section of the book of Ruth described the natural calmatives that struck in her life: a famine (Ruth 1:1), the death of her husband (Ruth 1:3), and the loss of her two sons who would be her only means of support after the passing of her husband (Ruth 1:5). The "insurance agent" inside of Naomi assessed her problems as "acts of God" and claimed that God afflicted her, "The Almighty hath dealt very bitterly with me. I went out full and the Lord hath brought me home again empty...the Almighty hath afflicted me." (Ruth 1:20-21) Because she was not walking in the revelation that she was a child of God as Paul described in Romans chapter eight, Naomi fell into an identity crisis and demanded that she be known as "Mara" – meaning "bitter." However, the narrator of the book of Ruth (the Holy Spirit) had a different idea about the woman in that he never referred to her as "Mara" but used her name "Naomi" – meaning "sweet" – twenty times in the short four-chapter book!

Naomi eventually began to recognize the blessing of God upon her life when she discovered that Ruth had stumbled upon the fields of her kinsman Boaz and had found favor in his eyes, "Naomi said unto her daughter in law, Blessed be he of the Lord, who hath not left off his kindness to the living and to the dead." (Ruth 2:20) The revelation continued to unfold until it brought the restoration of all that Naomi had lost and even more abundance, "And the women said unto Naomi, Blessed be the Lord, which hath not left thee this day without a kinsman, that his name may be famous in Israel.

And he shall be unto thee a restorer of thy life, and a nourisher of thine old age: for thy daughter in law, which loveth thee, which is better to thee than seven sons, hath born him." (Ruth 4:14-15) An old saying goes that we can either let hard times make us bitter or better. At first, Naomi chose to be bitter; however, as she began to see the hand of God at work, she realized that He had something better in store for her.

What a powerful lesson to learn and live by – the natural calamities that come upon us are not <u>acts of God</u>; however, the revelation that there is a greater one inside of us as sons and daughters of God does release <u>God to act</u> on our behalf.

There were present at that season some that told him of the Galilaeans, whose blood Pilate had mingled with their sacrifices. And Jesus answering said unto them, Suppose ye that these Galilaeans were sinners above all the Galilaeans, because they suffered such things? I tell you, Nay: but, except ye repent, ye shall all likewise perish. Or those eighteen, upon whom the tower in Siloam fell, and slew them, think ye that they were sinners above all men that dwelt in Jerusalem? I tell you, Nay: but, except ye repent, ye shall all likewise perish. (Luke 13:1-5)

In this short passage, Jesus addressed the issues that we have been dealing with for the past few chapters – people who suffer at the hands of others and those who suffer from natural disasters. Additionally, He suggested that it was in error to assume that these calamities had come upon them because of their sinfulness or "bad karma." However, Jesus threw us a "curveball" when He said – and even emphasized – that we must repent or perish.

Perhaps we may have been misinterpreting what He meant because we have not taken a serious look at the "trees" while trying to get an overview of the "forest." By that statement, I mean that perhaps we have taken His whole statement in one bite rather than biting off one word at the time to chew on. Therefore, let's take a couple paragraphs to look at the individual words in His admonition.

Let's start with the definition of "repent." Although it does carry the meaning of turning from sin and dedicating oneself to amending one's life and the emotion of feeling regret or contrition; "repent" also means to change one's mind. This is exactly what happened with Naomi – she changed her mind from focusing on all she had lost and blaming God for the tragedies in her life to thinking that God was actually at work and had a plan to bring restoration to her life.

The definition of "perish" means to destroy or ruin,

cause to cease to exist, deteriorate, or spoil. However, even when we have the right meaning, it may be possible that we have attributed that quality to the wrong source. I would assume that I'm not the only one who spent most of my life reading this statement to mean, "You need to feel regret and contrition so that you will turn from your sin and dedicate yourself to correcting your life; otherwise, God is going to judge you by destroying you, ruining you, causing you to cease to exist, deteriorating you, and spoiling you – and ultimately sending you to hell."

Let's consider an alternate way of reading this passage: When you suffer bad things at the hands of evil men or natural disasters, take time to change the way you think about what is happening to you. Rather than getting bitter, let God work inside of you to make you better. If you don't, the persecution from the outside and the bitterness from the inside will work together to totally destroy you – physically, emotionally, and spiritually.

If we read this directive from Jesus with this new approach to its meaning, we become what I like to call, "Martini Christians." Let me give you a minute to start breathing again, and I'll explain that I do not have any personal experience with martinis. All I know about the subject is one little statement that I picked up from a spy movie in which the secret agent used the ice cube in a drink to hide his listening device. In order to make sure that the instrument was not damaged, he instructed the bartender that the drink be stirred, not shaken.

There are a lot of things that can shake our worlds. Lucifer's fall shook the nations. (Isaiah 14:16; Ezekiel 26:15, 31:16) On the other hand, God shakes the heaven and the earth when He shows up. The scriptures confirm this point at least twenty times. (II Samuel 22:8; Job 9:6; Psalm 18:7, 18:7, 29:8 (two times), 46:3, 60:2, 68:8, 77:18; Isaiah 2:19, 2:21, 13:13, 24:18; Joel 3:16; Haggai 2:6, 2:21; Matthew 24:29; Mark 13:25; Hebrews 12:26) He shook the jail where Paul and Silas were incarcerated (Acts 16:26) and the house in which the disciples prayed (Acts 4:31). In addition, there are shakings that are still to come when God will shake nations (Haggai 2:7) and the very powers or stars of heaven (Luke 21:26, Revelation

40

6:13).

However, the general admonition in the scripture is that we are to come to a solid position in our faith so that nothing shakes us, "That ye be not soon shaken in mind, or be troubled, neither by spirit, nor by word, nor by letter as from us, as that the day of Christ is at hand." (II Thessalonians 2:2) Jesus likened those with a solid faith to a house that is built on a solid foundation that could not be shaken, "He is like a man which built an house, and digged deep, and laid the foundation on a rock: and when the flood arose, the stream beat vehemently upon that house, and could not shake it: for it was founded upon a rock." (Luke 6:48) Paul testified that his confidence in the Lord was immovable, "But none of these things move me, neither count I my life dear unto myself, so that I might finish my course with joy, and the ministry, which I have received of the Lord Jesus, to testify the gospel of the grace of God," (Acts 20:24) and David determined that he would ensure a similar unshakable relationship with the Lord, "I keep my eyes always is on the Lord.   With him at my right hand, I will not be shaken...Truly he is my rock and my salvation; he is my fortress, I will not be shaken." (Psalm 16:8, Psalm 62:6 – NIV)

The scriptures refer to stirrings that can come in our lives in both negative and positive ways. Bad emotions can stir us up: hatred (Proverbs 10:12), grievous words (Proverbs 15:1), wrath (Proverbs 15:18), pride (Proverbs 28:25), and anger (Proverbs 29:22). In the Old Testament we find the example of how Jezebel stirred up Ahab to do wickedness (I Kings 21:25) and in the New Testament we see how evil men stirred up hostilities against the early Christians (Acts 6:12, 12:18, 13:50, 14:2, 17:13, 19:23, 21:27).   On the other hand, the scriptures abound with examples of how stirring can be a good thing. The Lord stirred up His people to build the tabernacle. (Exodus 35:21, 35:26, 36:2) Centuries later, He stirred up Cyrus to fulfill the prophecy of returning the people of Israel to the land so they could rebuild the temple (II Chronicles 36:22, Ezra 1:1) and then stirred up Lord the people to do the work in the temple (Haggai 1:14).   In our own lives, we can be stirred up in our pure minds by the Word of God (II Peter 3:1), and we initiate our own stirring by acting in faith (Job 17:8; Psalm 35:23, 80:2; II Timothy 1:6; II Peter 1:13).

The bottom line is that we have no way of controlling what might happen in our lives; however, we do have control over how we are going to allow those things to affect us. We can be shaken, or we can be stirred. The basic difference is whether our lives are anchored on the solid foundation of who we are in Christ and who He is in us. Are we mature enough in Him and is He big enough in us so that we can pray <u>for</u> those who inflict injury upon us rather than to pray <u>about</u> the circumstances that find ourselves in? If not, we must repent – change the way we think – or else our circumstances will cause us to perish.

I've spent essentially the whole time up to this point dealing with the question of why bad things happen to good people; so, now it is time to consider why good things happen to bad people. But before we do any theological study on the point, I'd like to invite you to come with me to the island of Sri Lanka. A number of years ago, my wife and I arrived in the country to minister in a youth camp that had been arranged for the Christian high school and college students in that Buddhist state. When our host picked us up at the airport, he announced that we were going to have to cancel the retreat. He then went on to explain that the country was encountering a severe drought and that there was no water in the cisterns at the retreat center. Without water for cooking, cleaning, and drinking, it would be impossible to house the group at the camp. I explained that we had spent a lot of money in advance to cover the camp expenses and had flown all the way from America for the event. In my mind, it was impossible to cancel the retreat. There had to be a way to make it work. I asked for just twenty-four hours before he made his final decision. That night we asked the Lord for the windows of heaven to be opened in some miraculous way, and God answered our prayer in an even more dramatic way than we had anticipated. That night, we had the most horrendous rainstorm I have ever experienced. It didn't just "rain cats and dogs"; it was more like lions and wolves. I had never seen anything like it; the rain came down by the buckets full – no, barrels full. Not only did the cisterns fill to overflowing, the drought that was crippling the nation's agriculture was immediately alleviated. As a result, we were able to go forward with our plans for the retreat where we saw many young lives changed and destinies set. It wasn't until I revisited the nation almost thirty years later and was asked by one of the prominent pastors of the country to preach in his church that I saw proof of the remaining effect of the night that the windows of heaven were opened. That pastor, who is now a significant leader in the country, was called into the ministry as a high school student in that camp that would have been canceled had God not opened the windows of heaven.

Okay, so what does that have to do with good things happening to bad people? Well, I don't want to randomly lump the entire population of Sri Lanka in the category of "bad people"; however, we must remember that the vast majority of the population are Buddhists and that most of the rest are Hindus. Maybe they are good moral, honest, kind people human beings; however, in that they are not Christian believers, they don't qualify for the biblical definition of "good." God could have sent the rain specifically on the campground that we had rented for the conference, and that would have been a miraculous answer to my prayer; however, He sent the rains over the entire island and broke the draught that would have devastated the crops that year and forced the country's subsistence farmers into bankruptcy and even starvation.

Even though we have Old Testament biblical examples of God's discriminating between the believers and unbelievers (Genesis 26:1-14; Exodus 8:22-23, 9:4-7, 9:25-26, 10:23, 12:12-13), the New Testament principle is that He allows the blessings that He intends for His people to spill over on the unbelievers around them. In the account of Paul's shipwreck, we read the message of the angel that appeared to the apostle, telling him that his life would be preserved and that the added blessing would be that everyone on the ship would survive because of him. In spite of the fact that he could be sentenced to death if he allowed the prisoners to escape, the Roman guard jeopardized his own life by allowing all inmates to try to swim to safety – simply because he wanted to save the life of the apostle and had to spare everyone in order to rescue just one. It was a miraculous fulfillment of God's plan to extend the blessing of righteous Paul to the ungodly prisoners and crew on the ship with him. (Acts 27:23-44)

Let's get back to the discussion of the rain by noticing that Jesus Himself used rain to illustrate the principle of extending blessings to the unjust as well as to the just.

44

But I say unto you, Love your enemies, bless them that curse you, do good to them that hate you, and pray for them which despitefully use you, and persecute you; That ye may be the children of your Father which is in heaven: for he maketh his sun to rise on the evil and on the good, and sendeth rain on the just and on the unjust. For if ye love them which love you, what reward have ye? do not even the publicans the same? (Matthew 5:44-46)

Notice that the context in which He made this reference is that of an obligation upon believers to love, pray for, and bless those that would be considered their enemies – a principle that we have already discovered as an essential element in dealing with the bad things that come into our lives. In other words, the reason that good things happen in the lives of bad people is that New Testament believers – with new natures produced by the regenerative work of the Holy Spirit – have finally taken on the heart of God and the nature of Christ who prayed, even as the executioners were nailing Him to the cross, "Father, forgive them; for they know not what they do." (Luke 23:34)

I've heard Christians comment – and even pray – about unsaved friends or relatives that God should strip them of all their prosperity and even take away their health in an attempt to make them desperate enough to call out to God for intervention and salvation. Although the idea that when everything is taken away and you have nowhere else to look except up to God may sound like a logical approach, it is actually contradictory to the divine system. God's plan for bringing men to Himself is the old honey-versus-vinegar system for catching flies, "Despisest thou the riches of his goodness and forbearance and longsuffering; not knowing that the goodness of God leadeth thee to repentance?" (Romans 2:4)

In fact, the VERY best of all things in the history of the human race was done for the VERY worse of the people in every generation:

45

God commendeth his love toward us, in that, while we were yet sinners, Christ died for us...For if, when we were enemies, we were reconciled to God by the death of his Son, much more, being reconciled, we shall be saved by his life. (Romans 5:8-10)

Teach All Nations Mission

Teach All Nations Mission (TAN) is a global evangelical educational ministry birthed from the teaching ministries of Delron and Peggy Shirley. The name for Teach All Nations Mission was chosen to carefully indicate the exact heart of the Shirleys' mission. TAN's commitment is to establish a solid biblical foundation in national pastors and leaders so they can help enrich their own people. This vision is being accomplished by holding national leadership conferences and publishing and distributing Christian teaching materials in English and their local languages.

Someone accurately observed concerning the revival that is occurring in many parts of our world today that it is a mile wide but only an inch deep – the result of energetic evangelism by both missionaries and local Christians. Sadly, there is a marked shortage of teachers who are taking the next step in fulfilling our Lord's directive to teach them how to observe all that He has commanded. Therefore, Teach All Nations Mission has literally taken the words of Christ from Matthew 28:19, "Teach all nations," as its motto and mission statement.

TAN's commitment is to deepen that revival by training the pastors and leaders who then go back and strengthen their congregations. TAN pays for the travel and lodging of handpicked leaders because Delron and Peggy want to invest into their lives but know that these third-world saints could never afford to come at their own expense. TAN always provides the meals for all the guests during these conferences. The ministry also furnishes solid Christian literature in their local language or in English for those who understand the language.

Delron and Peggy realize that the challenge is much bigger than what they can accomplish in person; therefore, they have determined to expand the scope of their vision. One area of expansion includes a scholarship fund that will allow selected individuals to obtain a formal education in solid Christian colleges and Bible schools or through correspondence courses. The ministry has also assisted in building a Christian school in Zimbabwe and a Bible college in Nepal. Additionally, Teach All Nations assists the pastors and leaders they work with in times of need such as the tsunami in Sri Lanka, the earthquake in Nepal, and hurricanes in Belize and in the Turks and Caicos Islands.

Your gifts to and prayers for Teach All Nations will help the Shirleys continue their outreach to Christian leadership around the world.

Teach All Nations Mission
3210 Cathedral Spires
Colorado Springs, CO 8904
719-685-9999
www.teachallnationsmission.com
teachallnations@msn.com

A New Dawn Rises – Rethinking Christian Struggles
(the second volume in the Non-Conformer's Trilogy)

In <u>A New Dawn Rises</u>, Bible teacher Dr. Delron Shirley examines the accounts of some of the great spiritual struggles in the Bible from Jacob's all-night wresting match with an angel to Jesus' agonizing three hours in the Garden of Gethsemane. The conclusions that he draws from these stories can change the way that you view life and all the challenges it may bring your way.

Becoming a Person of Legacy
(the third volume in the Non-Conformer's Trilogy)

Someone once said that the two most important days of a person's life are the day he is born and the day he discovers why he was born. Each of us has a divine destiny that God has orchestrated since before we were even born. Unfortunately, most people live their whole lives without actually finding – much less, fulfilling that purpose. In <u>Becoming a Person of Legacy</u>, discover how to make your life leave a lasting impact.

Bingo – A Fresh Look at Grace

An old joke tells of a man who stood at the Pearly Gates recounting all his good deeds in an effort to gain entry into Paradise. When Saint Peter tallied up the gentleman's score, he did not have anywhere near enough points to qualify. His knee-jerk reaction to the count was, "I'll never get in except by the grace of God." At that instant, the gates swung open and Saint Peter graciously welcomed the gentleman inside. We all know that it is only through grace that we will ever inherit the kingdom of God, but how much do we understand about this all-important subject? Join Bible teacher Delron Shirley as he explores the biblical principle of grace and investigates some of the misconceptions that are current in the Body of Christ today.

Christmas Thoughts

Christmas. The very mention of the word fills our hearts and heads with thoughts – joyous memories, visions of childhood delights, scenes of family gatherings, smells of fresh pastries, tastes of delicious holiday treats, recollections of special friends, strains of favorite carols, and "warm fuzzies" of evergreens, mistletoe, roaring fires, fancy wrappings, shiny decorations, and happy faces. Yes, Christmas is all about thoughts. And we invite you to snuggle up with a hot chocolate and delve into our thoughts about Christmas – and the Christ child whose coming we are celebrating.

Cornerstones of Faith

In our Christian faith, there are some important cornerstones which serve as foundations to bear the weight of the life we are to build upon them, as indicators or identifiers of who we are as believers, as ceremonial testimonies to the fact that our lives are being built upon Christ, and as unquestionable and invariable standards against which to test and measure everything else in our lives. Proper attention to these essential cornerstones of our faith ensure that our lives rest upon a firm foundation so that we will not fail or falter. Join Delron Shirley in an examination of the foundation on which our lives must be built.

Daily Devotional Bible Study (five volumes)

This five-volume set of studies takes you on a four-year journey through the Bible. Each manual consists of a walk through the scripture based on studying one chapter each weekday for the fifty-two weeks in a year. Each daily entry includes one verse to memorize. Next comes a short distillation of the basic principle of the chapter and a brief outline of the chapter. This study is intended to be of a rather devotional approach. The Bible study is followed by a simple prayer intended to bring the truth of the chapter into practical application. A section for the reader's notes follows where you can log your own personal revelations and insights about the chapter. A space for logging your own personal spiritual journal (which could include prayer requests, answered prayers, and testimonies) rounds out the daily devotion. The entries for the weekends are a similar format for a study through Psalms. Just twenty minutes a day, seven days a week, fifty-two weeks a year will produce one brand new man in each individual who seriously applies himself to the program and the program to himself.

Daily Ditties from Delron's Desk (Six issues are available)

Each new day comes with its own challenges and blessings. In Daily Ditties from Delron's Desk, you'll enjoy a little pick-me-up to get your day started. So sit back with a warm cup of coffee or tea and see what is in store for you today.

Good People, Bad Things, and Vice Versa
(the first volume in the Non-Conformer's Trilogy)

One of the most difficult questions that has challenged ordinary men and the world's greatest thinkers and philosophers throughout the ages has been, "Why do bad things happen to good people and why do good things happen to bad people?" The answer to this conundrum lies in simply reprograming the way we think about inequity and the divine order of things. Join Bible teacher Dr. Delron Shirley as he explores the biblical truths that will help unravel this mystery.

Lessons from the Life of David

Michelangelo's famous sculpture David in the Piazza Signoria in Florence, Italy, has often been noted as a most perfect depiction of the human body. And we often think of its subject – the biblical David – as being perfect as well. However, the wonderful thing about the Bible is that it tells

51

the truth – even about its greatest heroes. They are presented to us as uncovered as Michelangelo's subject, with the only difference being that the Bible depicts its subjects with all their warts, mid-rib bulges, scars, and other defects. In Lessons from the Life of David, Bible teacher Delron Shirley explores both David's triumphs and failures in order to find valuable lessons for our own lives for today.

The Great Commission – DOABLE

While traversing the teeming streets of Kathmandu, Nepal, missionary teacher Delron Shirley was overwhelmed with the throngs of people who had not yet heard the gospel of Jesus Christ. Looking out at the myriad of faces, it seemed like an impossible task to reach them all. Yet, he knew that Jesus' directive was that the gospel be taken to every human—not just in this one city, but on the entire planet. If reaching this one city seemed like a gargantuan challenge, reaching the planet was beyond imagination! Join Delron in his quest through the scriptures as he explores why the Bible promises that the Great Commission can actually be accomplished and how it is doable in our generation.

Dr. Livingstone, I Presume

Probably the most famous quote in all the annals of missionary history is the greeting of newsman and adventurer Henry Stanley when he finally reached missionary and explorer David Livingstone in the remote interior of Africa, "Dr. Livingstone, I presume?" In this little study based on that historic encounter, Bible teacher and missionary Dr. Delron Shirley considers how we can really pick out who is a missionary. His real hope is that you can find yourself in these few short pages and join the call to fulfill the Great Commission of bringing the gospel of Jesus Christ to the whole world in this generation.

Finally, My Brethren

"Finally, my brethren," these are words that seem all too
52

familiar to us when we think of putting on the armor of God for spiritual warfare. However, we often miss the real impact of Paul's message to the church because we have used this as our starting point. But just as we don't start at the top step when we climb a ladder, we can't begin our preparation for spiritual warfare at the last step – putting on the armor. In fact, the Apostle Paul gave us more than fifty steps of preparation to complete before we are ready to get dressed for battle. Join Delron Shirley as he uncovers these often neglected truths. Discover life-transforming truths about your enemy, yourself, God, who you are in Christ, who Christ is in you, and your position in the struggle between the powers of heaven and hell.

Going Deeper in Jesus

In this seventy-three-day devotional volume, Bible teacher Delron Shirley invites you to go with him on a quest into the Jesus treasure chest to discover the unimaginable gifts that God has made available to us in Christ.

The IN Factors

It was offering time in the Sunday school class, and the teacher directed the children to quote a Bible verse about giving as they dropped in their nickels and dimes. A little Afro-American girl with her hair in meticulously cornrow braids grinned from ear to ear as she dropped in the first coin and quoted, "It is more blessed to give than to receive." Her redheaded, freckle-faced friend shyly blushed as she added to the coffer while mumbling, "Give and it shall be given back to you." Next, a young guy tossed in what might have been his "tooth fairy money" as he flashed a broad smile that exposed the spot where his front tooth had been last Sunday. He then recited, "The Lord loves a cheerful giver." As the fourth little fellow stumbled through, "The seed in the good soil brought forth thirty-, sixty-, and one-hundred-fold return," the teacher anxiously eyed the next child – a first-time visitor who had not been schooled in any of the "giving" passages. Anxious over the fact that the guest would be

53

embarrassed, her heart raced a bit as the offering basket reached him. As the reluctant little tyke begrudgingly plunked in his contribution, he blurted out, "A fool and his money are soon parted." Although the visitor's quote wasn't from the Bible, it was apparently more appropriate in his own case than any of the verses with which the teacher had coached the rest of the pupils. The truth is that most of us, like the students in the elementary class, have been taught only part of the lesson of what God wants us to know about finances. In The IN Factors, Bible teacher Delron Shirley invites you to join him as he explores some of the lessons that have been taught – but equally important – truths on the topic.

In This Sign Conquer

Marching toward an enemy that he wasn't sure he could defeat, Constantine questioned himself, his army, his military abilities, and even his deities. Then suddenly something happened that changed his life. No, something happened that changed the whole history of Western civilization. He saw a vision in the sky of the Christian cross accompanied by the words, "In this sign conquer." Abandoning his pagan gods and accepting the cross of Christ as his battle insignia, he marched into the Battle of Malvian, defeated Maxentius, and took the throne of the Roman Empire. Since none of us was there in AD 312, we can't be certain how sincere the new emperor was in his acceptance of the cross as his victory symbol. However, we must know that there are signs and symbols that God has given to each of us to ensure our victory and success in life. Join Bible teacher Delron Shirley as he explores this fascinating topic.

Interface

This book should be viewed as an anthology because each of the seven studies was written at a different time with no deliberate connection to the other six. However, there is a thread running through these independent studies that ties them all together as they communicate different aspects of one unified message – being strategic in our spirituality. The first study deals directly with the interfaces discussed in the Bible where we connect with the world around us, the kingdom of heaven, and the kingdom of darkness. The second study in the series discusses finding the sensitive balance between two necessary interfaces – our need to spend time with God and our mandate to rise up and interact with the world. The third and fourth studies have to do with the biblical truths that we need to understand in order to accurately interface with our God, our world, and ourselves. In the letters to the seven churches of Asia Minor recorded in Revelation chapters two and there, only one of the churches is specifically mentioned as being at an interface; the church at Philadelphia is said to have an open door set before it. Interestingly, this is also the only church that is specifically mentioned as having a relationship with the Word of God. (Revelation 3:8, 10) The fifth study takes us through the life of one of our most beloved biblical heroes—David, the shepherd boy who killed a giant and wrote beautiful psalms. Although his life was riddled with one failure after another, he somehow attained the report that he was a man after God's own heart, which is the key to opening the doors of interface with the world that we learn about in the letter to the Philadelphian church. (Revelation 3:7) Next, we look at what it really means to have a heart after the very heart of God – one that Bob Pierce, founder of World Vision, described as being broken with the same things that break the heart of God. Finally, the book concludes with a challenge to never fall short of the opportunities and blessing that God has provided for us as we interface with the One who sent us and those with whom we are to interface.

Israel – Key to Human Destiny

The Jewish people and the nation of Israel are puzzles and enigmas in world politics and human logic. How can it be that a group of people who account for less than one half of a percent of the world's population is responsible for one out of every five Nobel Peace prizes? Israel is so tiny a territory that no world map can even squeeze its name on the space allotted it on the layout, yet this minuscule nation dominates our evening news every night. Why is it that one little country of only a few million people can tie up the wealth, the foreign policy, and the political movements of the greatest nations on the face of the earth? Why is it that of all the ethnic groups in the world, only one bears the stigma (or honor) of having its name specifically coined into a word of hate and antagonism: anti-Semitism? The answers to these puzzling questions lie in the fact that these are no ordinary people and this is no ordinary piece of real estate. These are covenant people living in covenant land. Their destiny is charted by prophetic words from God Himself. Indeed, the saga of all mankind revolves around this people. Israel is the key to the human drama. Join Delron Shirley as he journeys into the past and glimpse into the future in order to understand the present.

The Last Enemy

Fear? Death? Defeated!! The Bible declares that death is our ultimate enemy and that the fear of death is a cruel warden that can hold us in the chains of slavery and bondage throughout our lives. BUT, our enemy Death has met his Waterloo and can no longer hold us in his power. In The Last Enemy, explore Passover weekend AD 33 changed your destiny.

Lessons Along the Way

Welcome to a journey that will lead you across the towering Himalayan Mountains, over rushing waterfalls, and into your own backyard. At each step of the journey and around each bend in the path, you will discover the most exciting thrills of life – not the rush of adrenalin released while crashing through the rapids of the Grand Canyon, not the spine-tingling chill of coming face-to-face with demonic supernatural forces, not the awesome hush of grandeur inspired by the majestic sunsets across the glacier polish of the majestic Sierra Nevada range – although all these and much more are included. Rather, you will discover the thrill

56

of hearing the voice of God Himself speaking to you for direction and encouragement. Join us on this fascinating journey through life. Be ready to learn all the lessons along the way!

Living for the End Times

"The end is near!" "Jesus is coming back!" "These are the last days!" We all have heard these prophecies. Sometimes, we've heard them so often and over such a long period of time that they may have lost their impact. Yes, we believe that these are the last days, but we somehow keep living as if we think that things will always keep going as they always have and that nothing is ever going to change. Is it possible that we have given mental ascent to the concept of the end time but never let it really get hold of our lives? Let's explore what it means to live our lives as if we really believed that these are the end days – after all, they really are!

Maturing into the Full Stature of Jesus Christ

As a child, I learned a little song in children's church: "To be like Jesus, to be like Jesus. That's all I ask – just to be like Him." When I grew up, I realized that there was a whole lot more to becoming like Christ than just singing a little children's song. It has been said that going to church doesn't make you a Christian any more than sitting in the garage will make you an automobile or sitting in a donut shop will make you a policeman. There is a maturing process that we must go through if we ever hope to manifest the true nature of Christ in our lives. That maturing process demands that we have a total transformation in the way we think – that we be brainwashed, if you will. It requires more than just saying the right words; after all a parrot can speak English, but he is not an Englishman. In the same way, we must not settle for just learning the Christian jargon; we must be transformed into the very likeness of Christ through the renewing of our mentalities. You may not be what you think you are, but what you think – YOU ARE! Join Bible teacher Delron Shirley as he investigates how the way we think determines who and what we will be. Learn how your thinking can transform you into the full stature of Jesus Christ.

Maximum Impact

He showed up totally unannounced with no publicity agent, no campaign manager, and no budget to fund a campaign. Yet within three short weeks, he established a viable community of faith that was soon acknowledged and recognized as a role model throughout the world. Who was this man, and how did he flip the world one hundred eighty degrees on its axis? Join Bible teacher Dr. Delron Shirley as he makes a fascinating quest into the man, his methods, and the mission of a man who left maximum impact everywhere he went.

Of Kings and Prophets – Shapers of the Destinies of Nations

Dr. Delron Shirley invites you to travel back through the corridors of time to visit the era of the Old Testament kings and prophets in the nations of Israel and Judah – the men who shaped the destinies of their nations. In walking through the encounters, interactions, and conflicts in the lives of these historical figures, we are constantly reminded of the words of the New Testament writer who said that everything that happened in the lives of these men serves as an example and a caution to us so we can make a difference in our own generation.

Passion for the Harvest – A Missions Handbook

We all know the Lord's statement that the harvest is plenteous but the laborers are few. However, I would like to suggest a little different consideration of the situation: the harvest is plenteous but the laborers are untrained. The cover photograph of a Nepali woman harvesting her grain not only pictures the primitive conditions in which the third world harvests their physical grain, it also helps us get a glimpse of the need for the entire Body of Christ to be trained for the spiritual harvest as well. Passion for the Harvest, explores some of the pertinent truths necessary for preparing us for the challenge of the harvest. Learn how to sow in order to reap an abundant harvest and how to discern the harvest that the Lord is sending your way. Learn how to develop the resourcefulness and the expectant hope necessary to stand steadfastly until the harvest manifests and we discover new truths concerning the tools and the stamina necessary for reaping the full harvest. In short, develop a passion for the harvest!

People Who Make a Difference

Have you ever noticed that there are some people who just seem to stand out from the crowd? Although they may seem ordinary in so many ways, there is just some special something about them that identifies them as unique individuals. Though they may not be the "movers and shakers" that we think of as the ones who can push their way to the top of the corporate ladder, they somehow wind up leaving an indelible mark on their worlds. Let's explore what it is that makes some people the ones who make a difference. Better yet, let's learn how to be those individuals!

Positioned for Blessing and Power

In the first Psalm, David gave us a formula for a life that qualifies for God's blessings – be careful about where you walk, sit, and stand. In the book of Ephesians, the Apostle Paul gave us a formula on how to live in the power and authority of God – be determinate about where we sit, walk, and stand. Bible teacher Delron Shirley combines these two principles – one from the Old Testament and one form the New – in a way that can revolutionize your life.

Problem People of the Bible

In Problem People of the Bible, you will meet many of the biblical characters you have had to skip over as you did your daily reading because you simply couldn't understand exactly how their lives figure into the message of God's love and plan of salvation. This insightful story will help you make sense of their place in the grand scheme of the Bible and the story of God's dealings with the human family.

So, You Wanna Be A Preacher

A distillation of Delron Shirley's twenty-five years of mentoring young ministers and the evaluation of over ten thousand church services and sermons, So You Wanna Be A Preacher covers a wide range of topics from how to recognize and respond to the call into the ministry to tips on preparing and presenting your sermons and on getting them published. Special emphasis is given to helping you understand the minister's job description and recognizing how to manifest the Holy Spirit's presence in your ministry. The minister's personal life – including discussion of ethics and etiquette – is a major focus in the study. No matter what your ministry or calling, you are guaranteed to get new insights in your role as a minister and gain some helpful hints into effectively serving the Lord and His people.

Tread Marks

Does your life leave a mark on the people you meet and the circumstances you find yourself in? In Tread Marks, you'll learn a number of where-the-rubber-meets-the-road principles of successful Christian living that are guaranteed to ensure that you will leave a positive impression on individuals and society. Based on biblical principles and true life experiences, this book grapples with everyday life issues and presents simple but effective approaches to facing them successfully and victoriously. From the stories of the sinking of the Titanic and an African safari adventures to the expositions on Joshua's conquest of the Promised Land and Joseph's rise from slavery to the second most powerful man in Egypt, you'll be entertained, inspired, and motivated. You'll discover how your life can make a lasting impression.

A Verse for the Day (Two Issues are available)

In A Verse for the Day, Bible teacher Delron Shirley brings you a new insight into the Word of God each day with observations about the unique contributions the selected verses can make in our lives. Though the studies of these verses are by no means comprehensive or exhaustive, the fresh insights you'll gain in these daily visits with the Word of God are guaranteed to encourage, challenge, and inspire you in your walk with the Lord.

Women for the Harvest

"God's secret weapon" – that's how many people are coming to realize that we, as women, are in the world of ministry. One example is, Dr. Yonggi Cho, who has the second largest church in the world. He has been quoted as saying, "Women are the greatest evangelistic tools. Someday the church will catch on." In this volume, author Peggy Shirley does an in-depth study into the history of why women have been forbidden from taking their God-given place in the church and explores the powerful biblical and historical examples of what happens when women are allowed to use the giftings which God has placed inside them. A revealing study of the scriptures which have long been used to block women from service, coupled with a motivational study on how to break free from the bondages which have held women back and a wealth of practical suggestions and advice -- this book is guaranteed to release you to become a true laborer in God's end-time harvest.

You'll be Darned to Heck if You Don't Believe in Gosh and Other Musings

This eclectic collection of mediations and musings addresses many issues concerning our Christian faith, including exactly what the Bible teaches about hell and who will go there, how prayer works, and how we should understand exactly who Jesus is. This study also takes you on a spiritual

61

journey that delves into such topics as simple advice for Christian leaders and the biblical formula for radical change – both in your own personality and in the complexion of a whole nation.

Lighthearted at times, but always simple and straight forward, this refreshing study makes discovering theological truths from the scripture fun and enlightening. Buckle your seatbelt as you join Bible teacher Delron Shirley as he journeys to such interesting places as Nepal and Nigeria in quest of spiritual insight and revelation. You'll be glad that you came along for the adventure as you discover many simple truths that have always seemed just too difficult to understand.

Your Home Can Survive in the 21st Century

Have you ever heard someone say that we should get rid of old fashion ideas about marriage, family, and morals and add "After all, it is the twenty-first century"? With the rapid decline in traditional values, we might actually begin to question if our home will be able to survive in this new century. But there is good news if we only recognize that what is happening to the family today is a prophetic attack by the forces of the devil and that we are well equipped to fight back and conquer! Dr. Delron Shirley says, "Your home can not only survive – it can thrive!!"

www.ingramcontent.com/pod-product-compliance
Lightning Source LLC
LaVergne TN
LVHW052339080426
835508LV00044B/2735